Mythical Mermaid Dot-to-Dot Book for Adults Puzzles From 150 to 750 Dots

By Laura's Dot to Dot Therapy

Copyright © 2018

How To Use This Book

Hi! We're so glad you're a lover of puzzles and dot connecting- we are too!

Connecting the dots in this book is simple- just relax and follow the numbers in consecutive order, drawing a straight line between each one. Dot 1 will connect to dot 2 and so on and so forth until there are no more dots to connect. There's always another dot and you'll always find it. Connect every dot to discover the beautiful images they create.

In case you get lost or can't find a dot, never stress- there's an answer key at the back of the book that will show you exactly where each dot connects to the next. If you want to color your images, we encourage you to do so! Feel free to try all different colors and coloring mediums for your images!

If you find any errors or omissions in this book, email us at _Laurasdottodot@gmail.com_ and please let us know! We want you to have the best dot to dot experience!

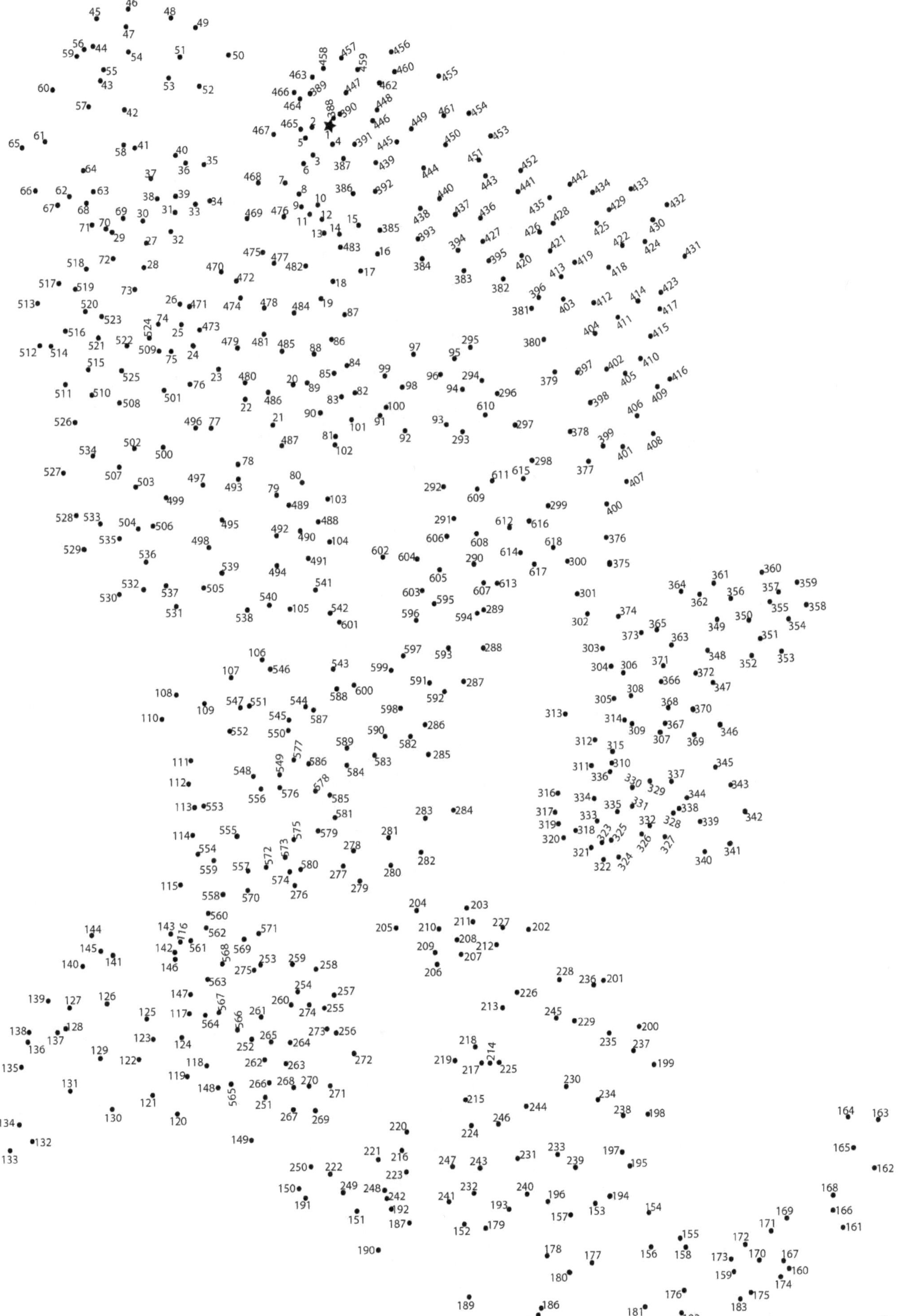

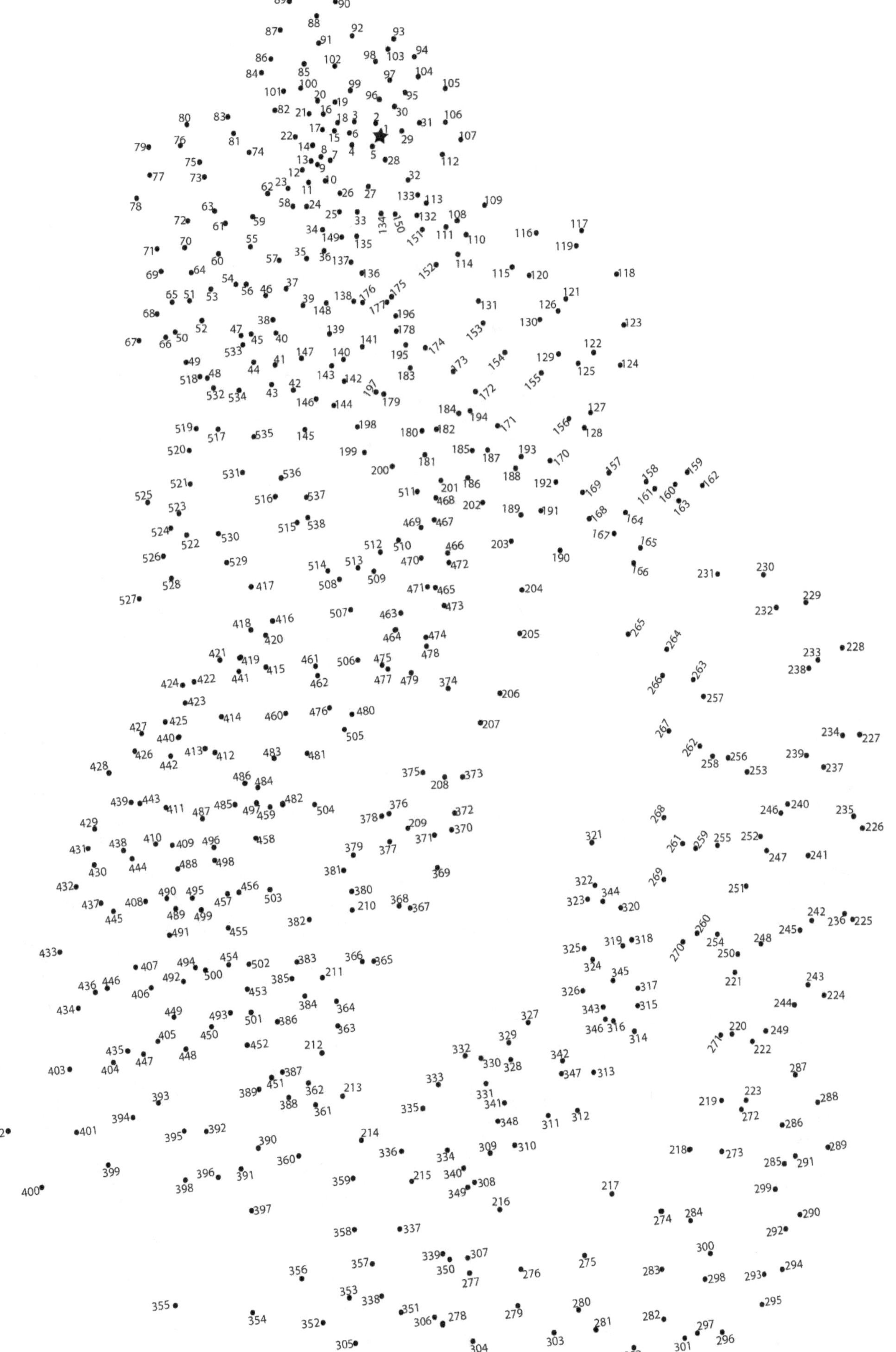

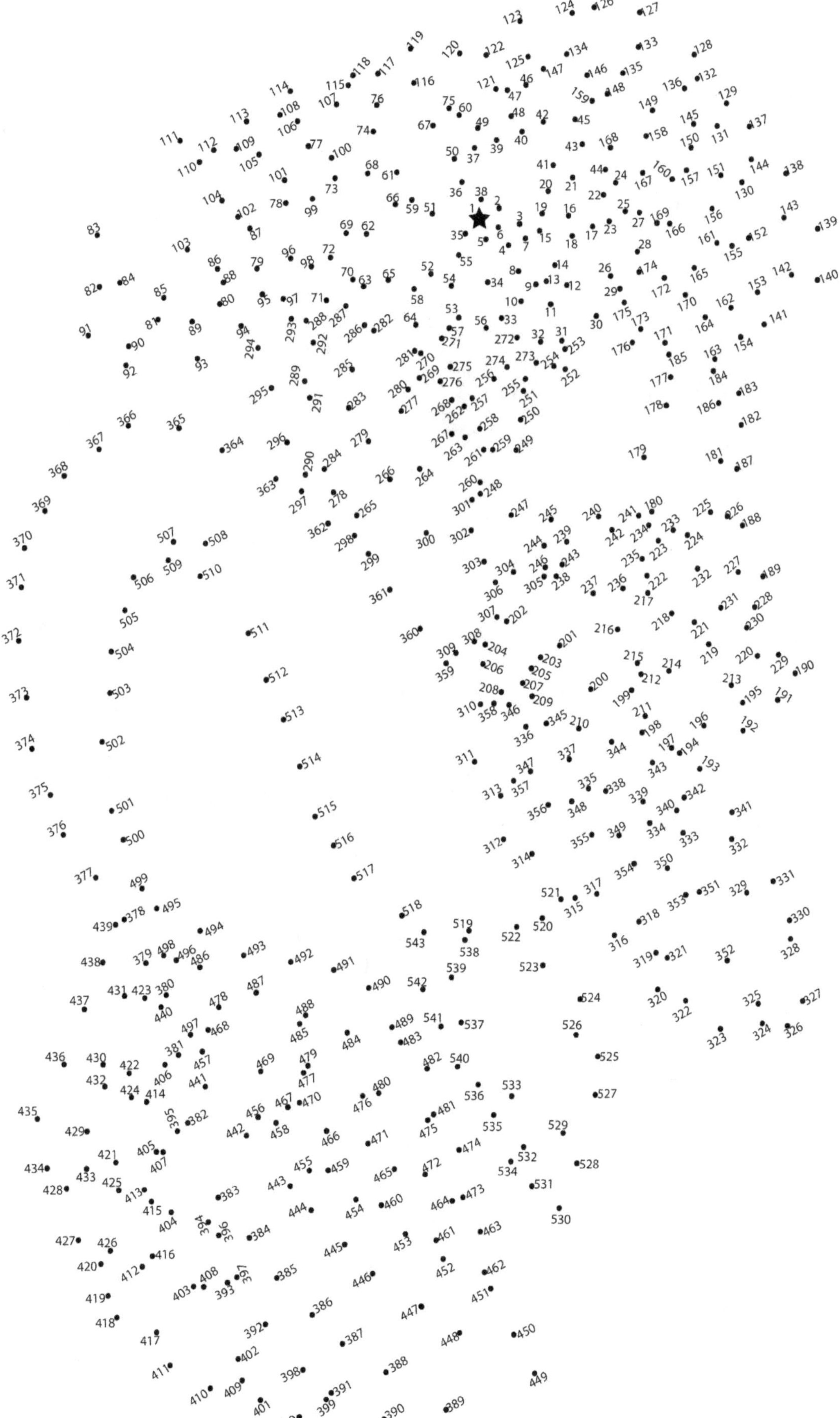

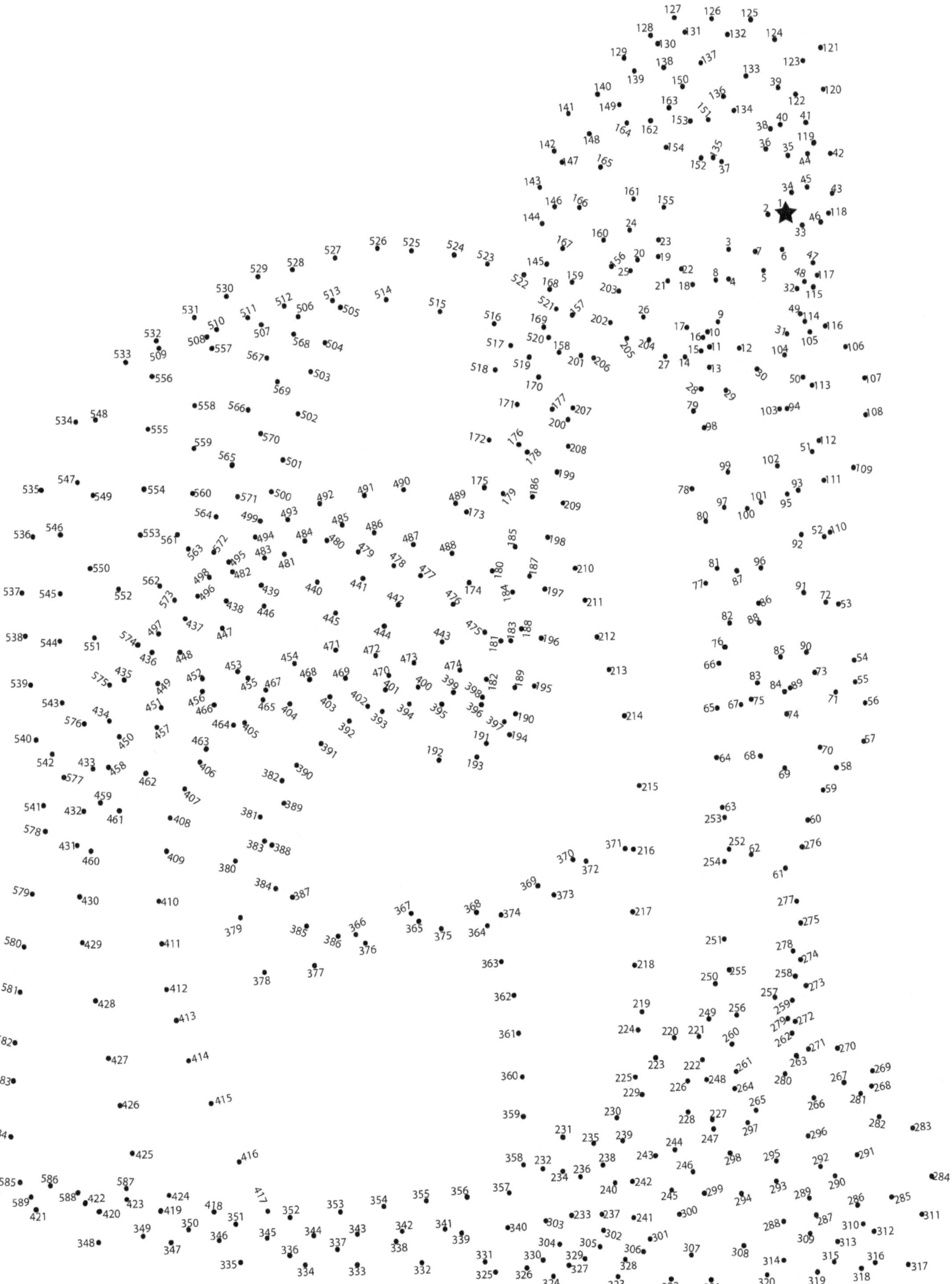

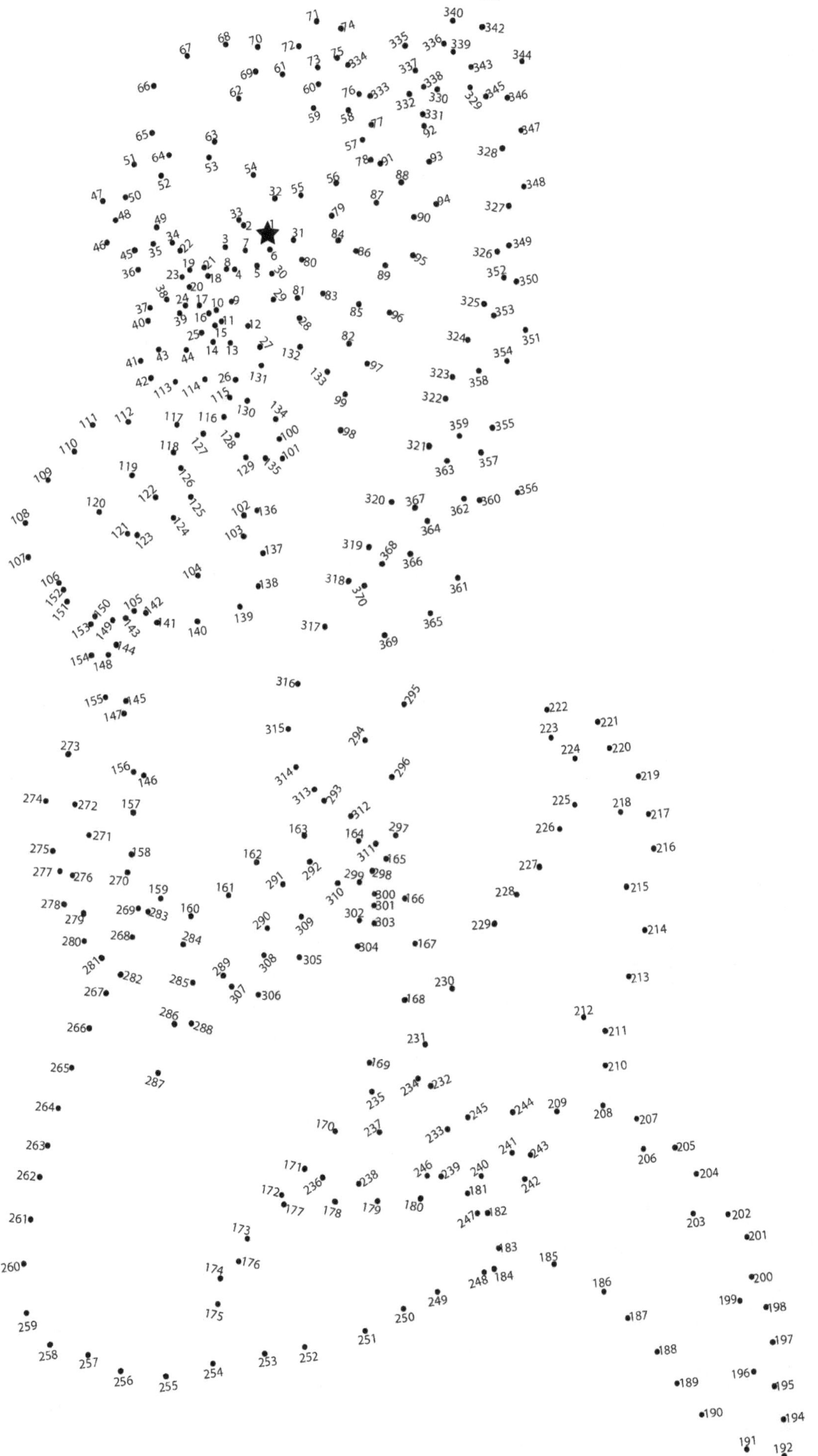

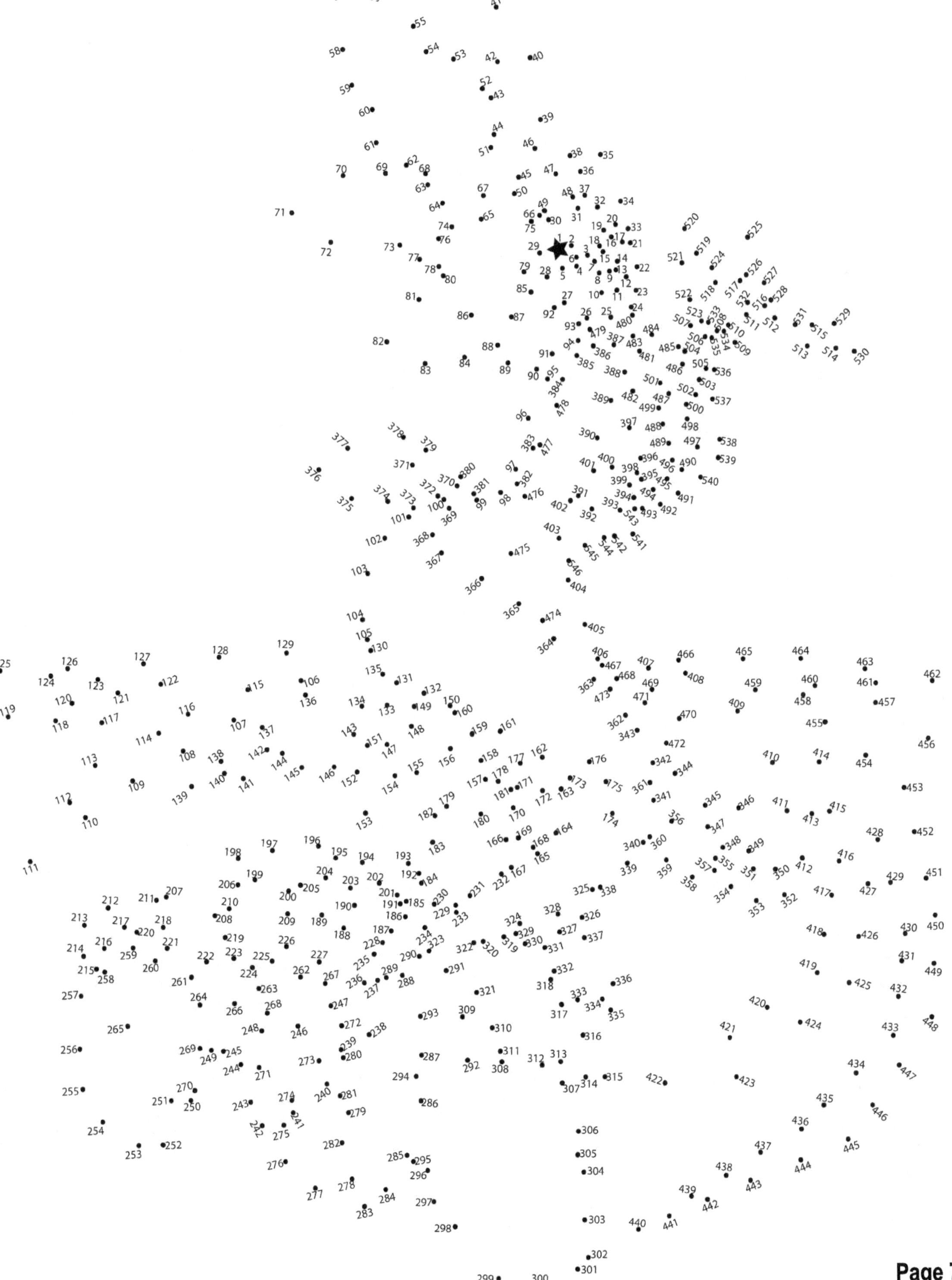

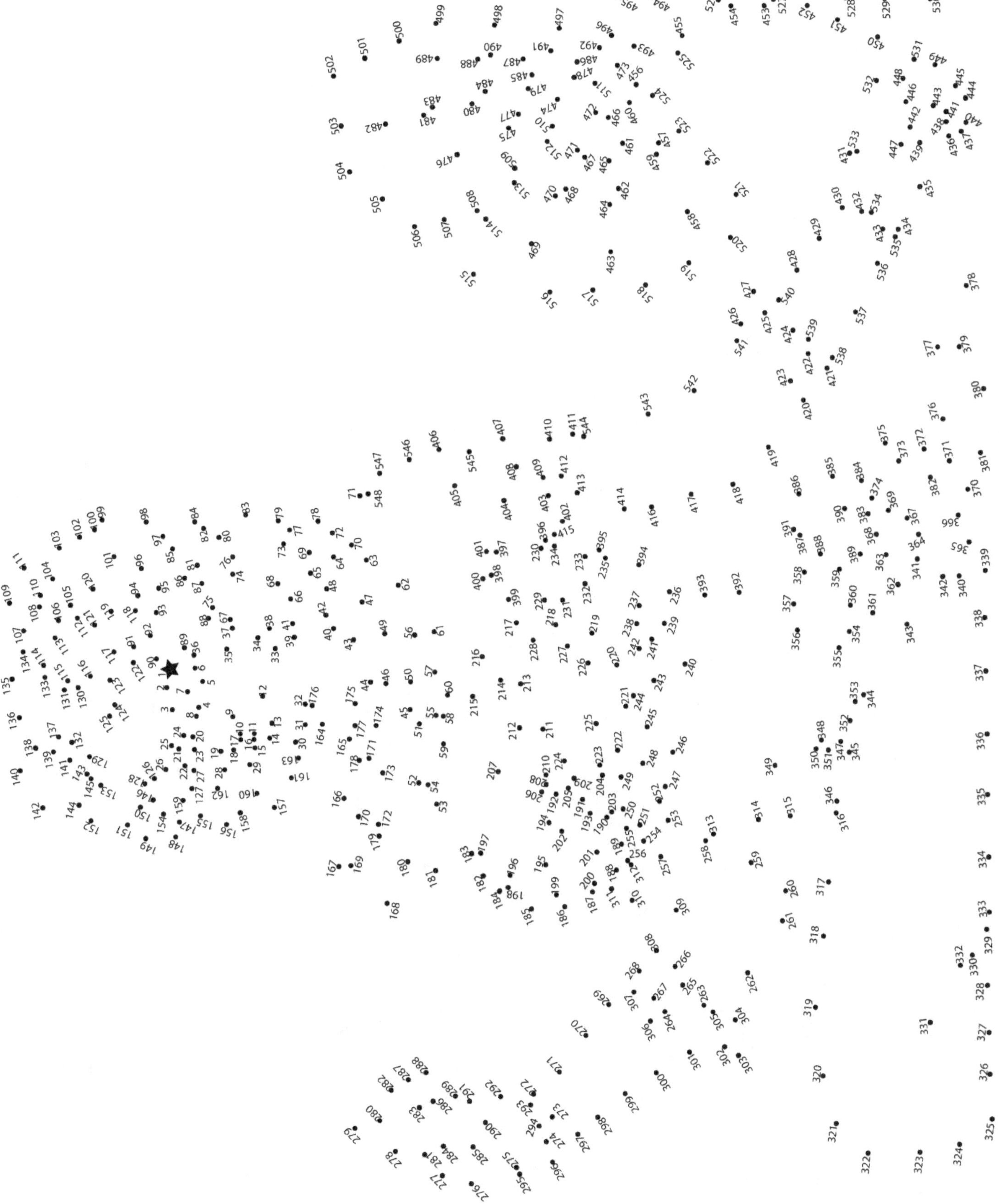

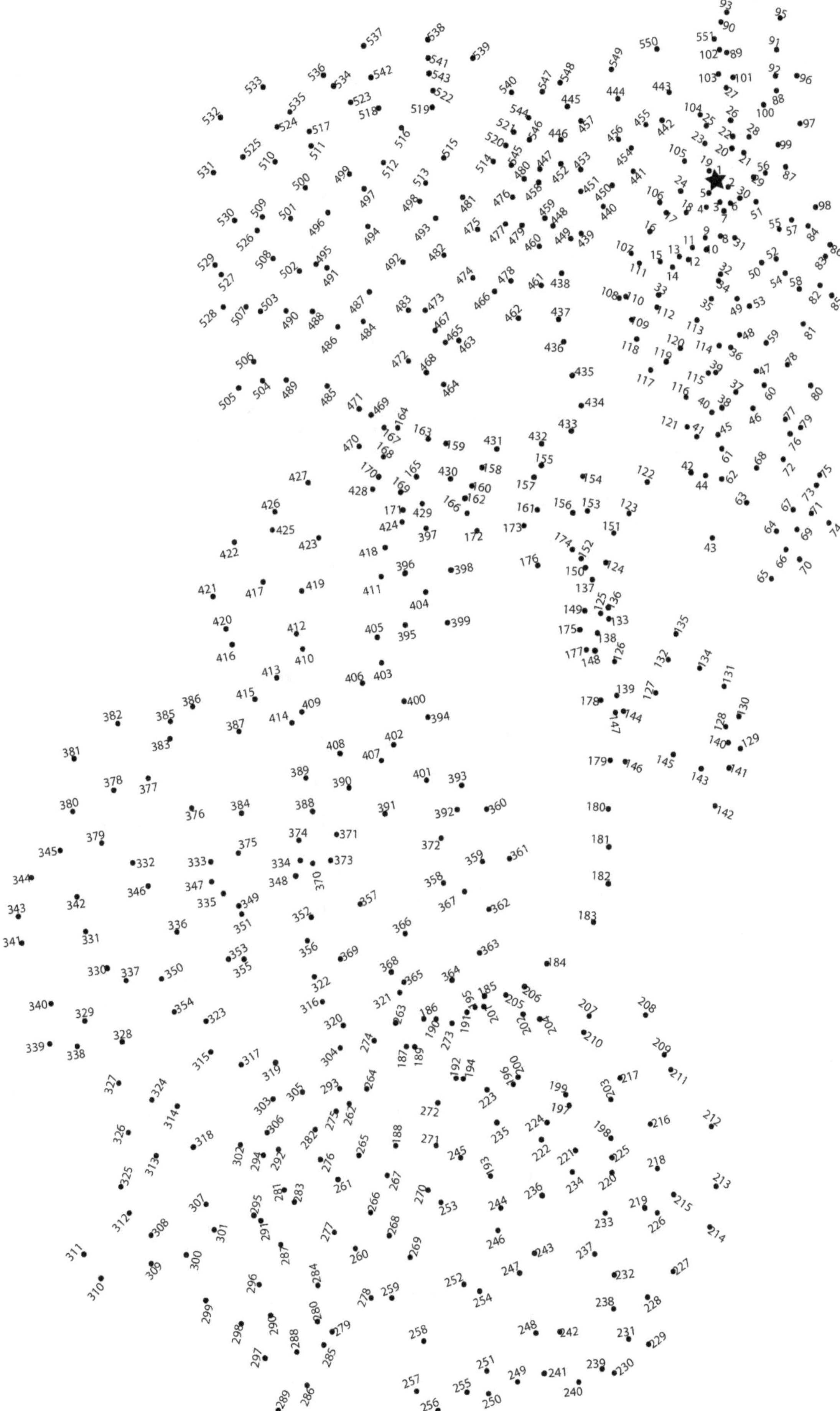

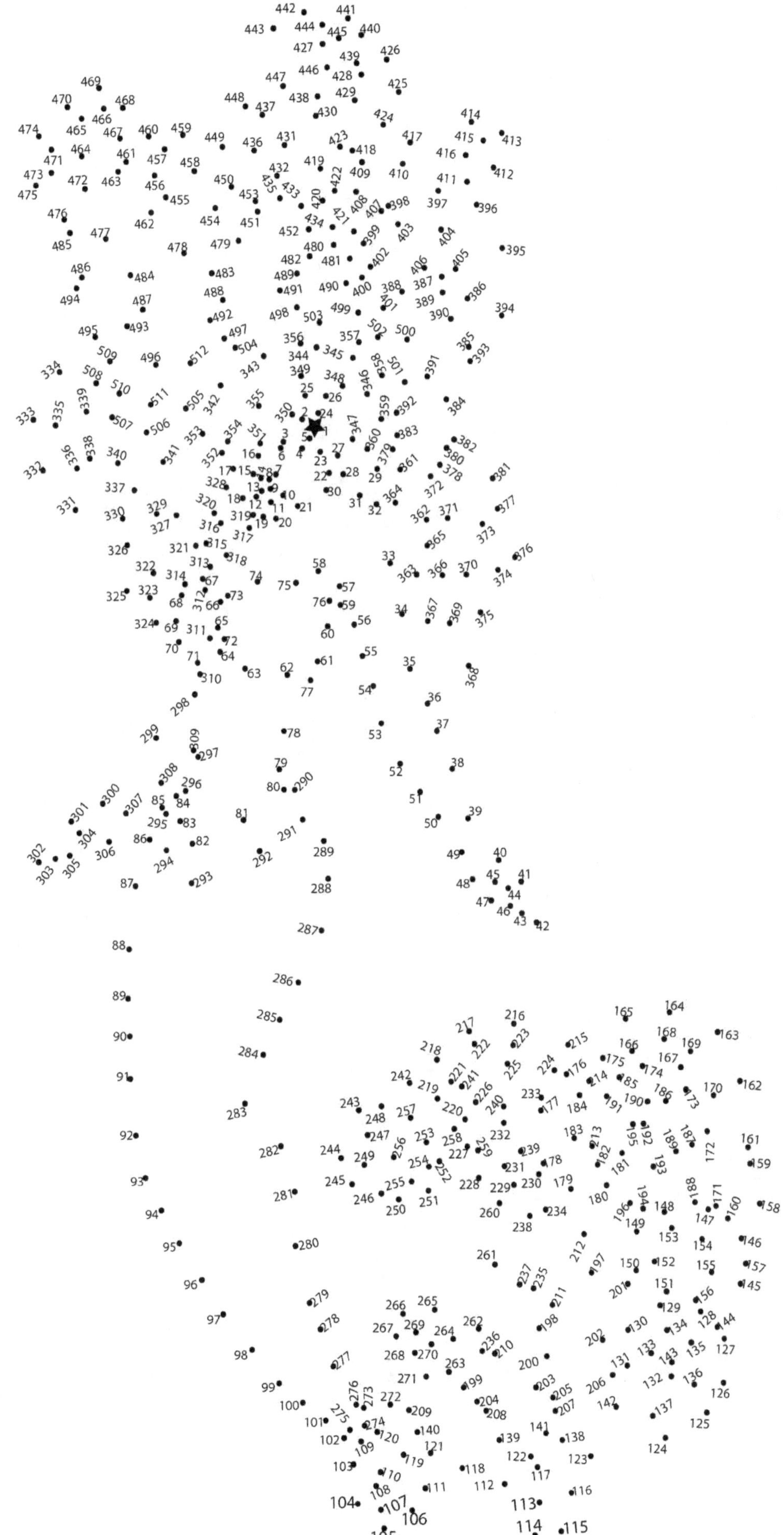

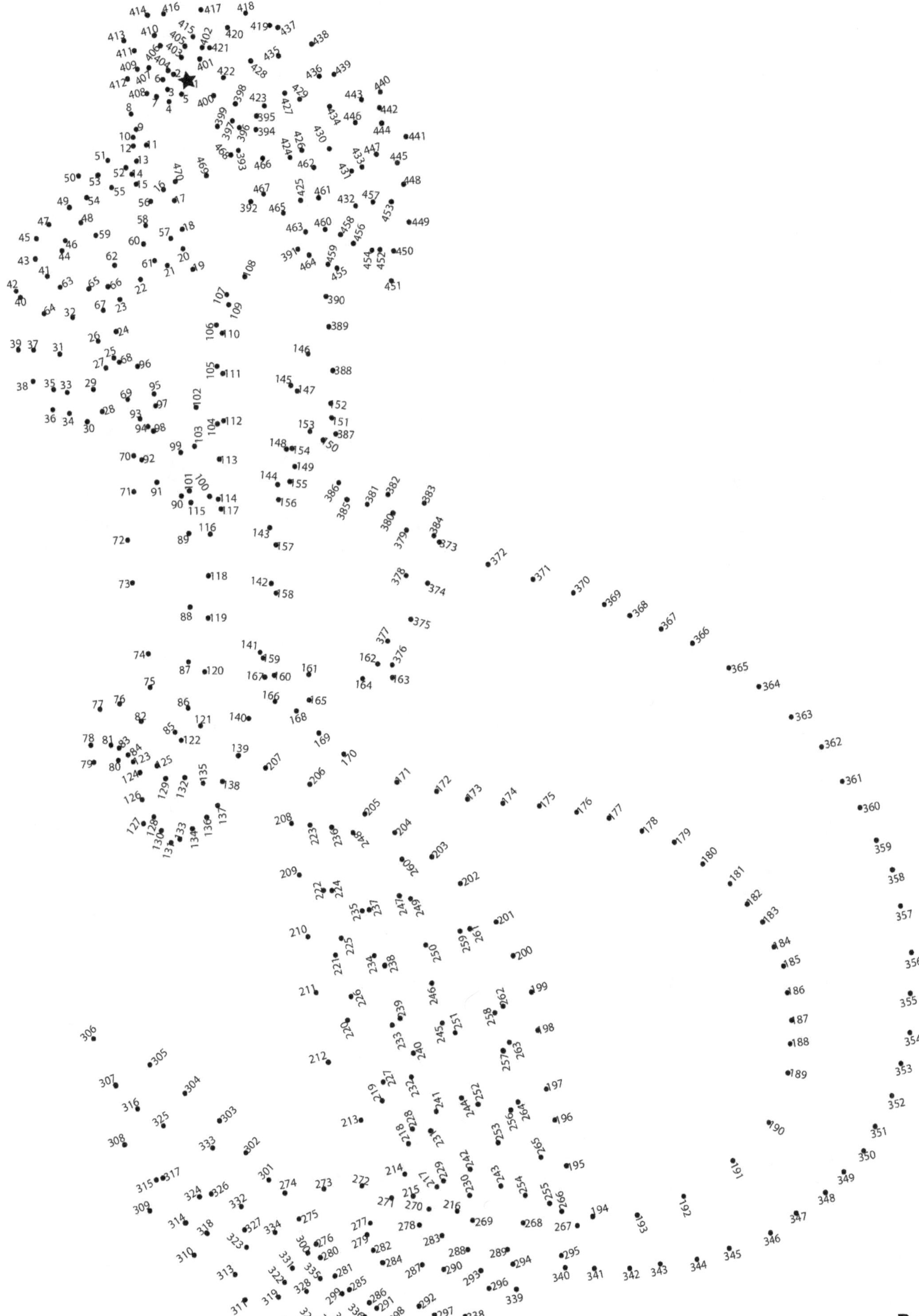

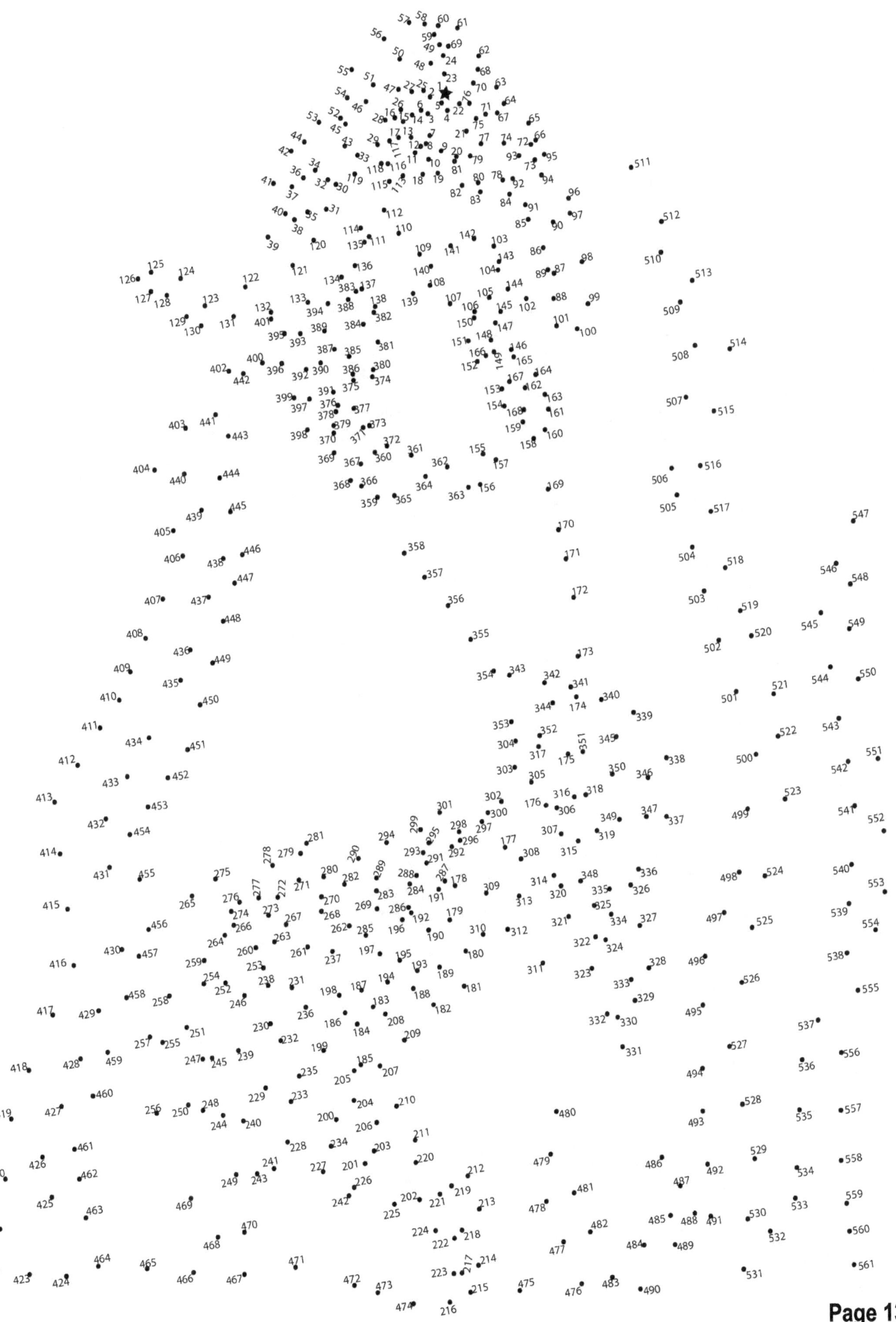

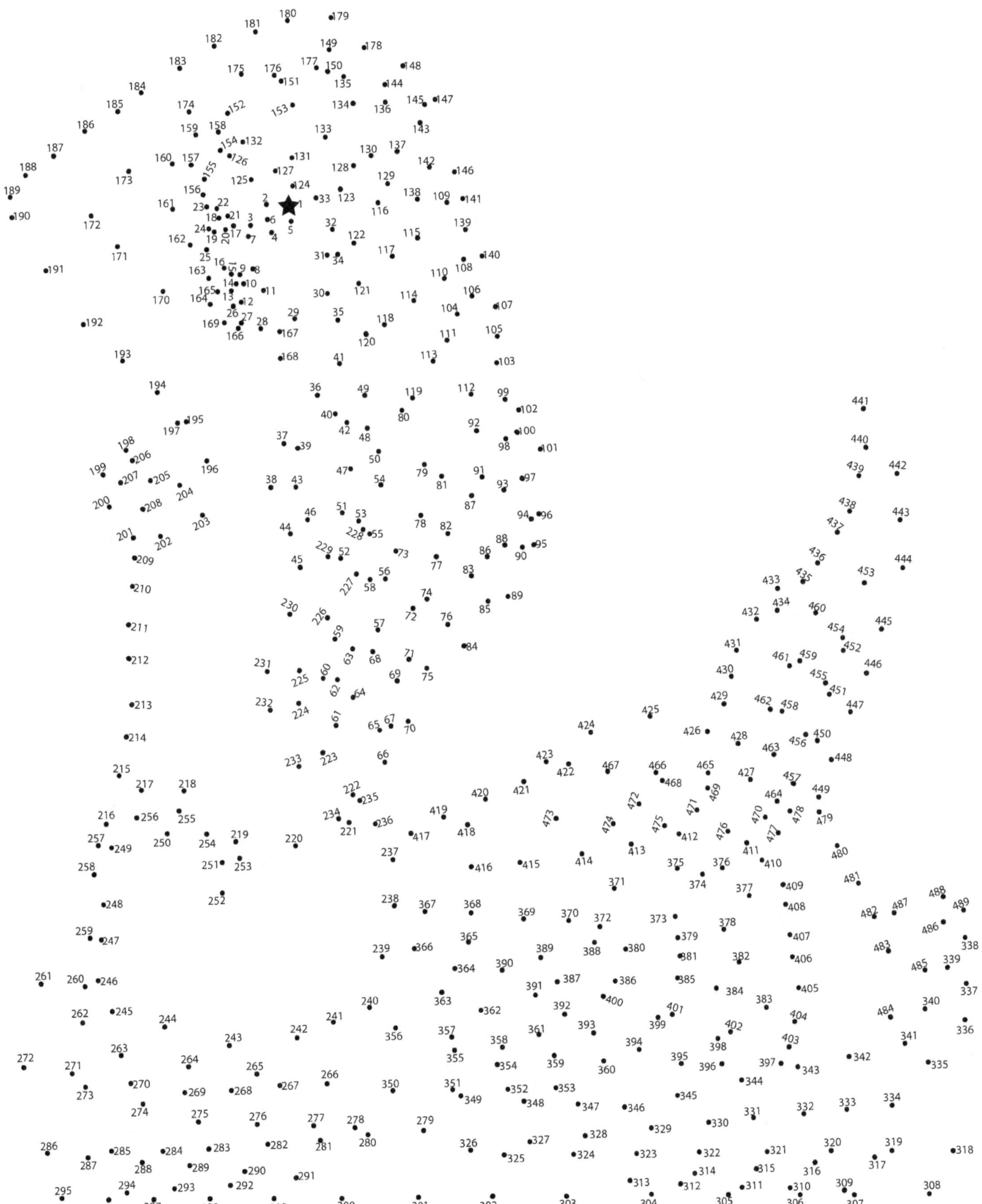

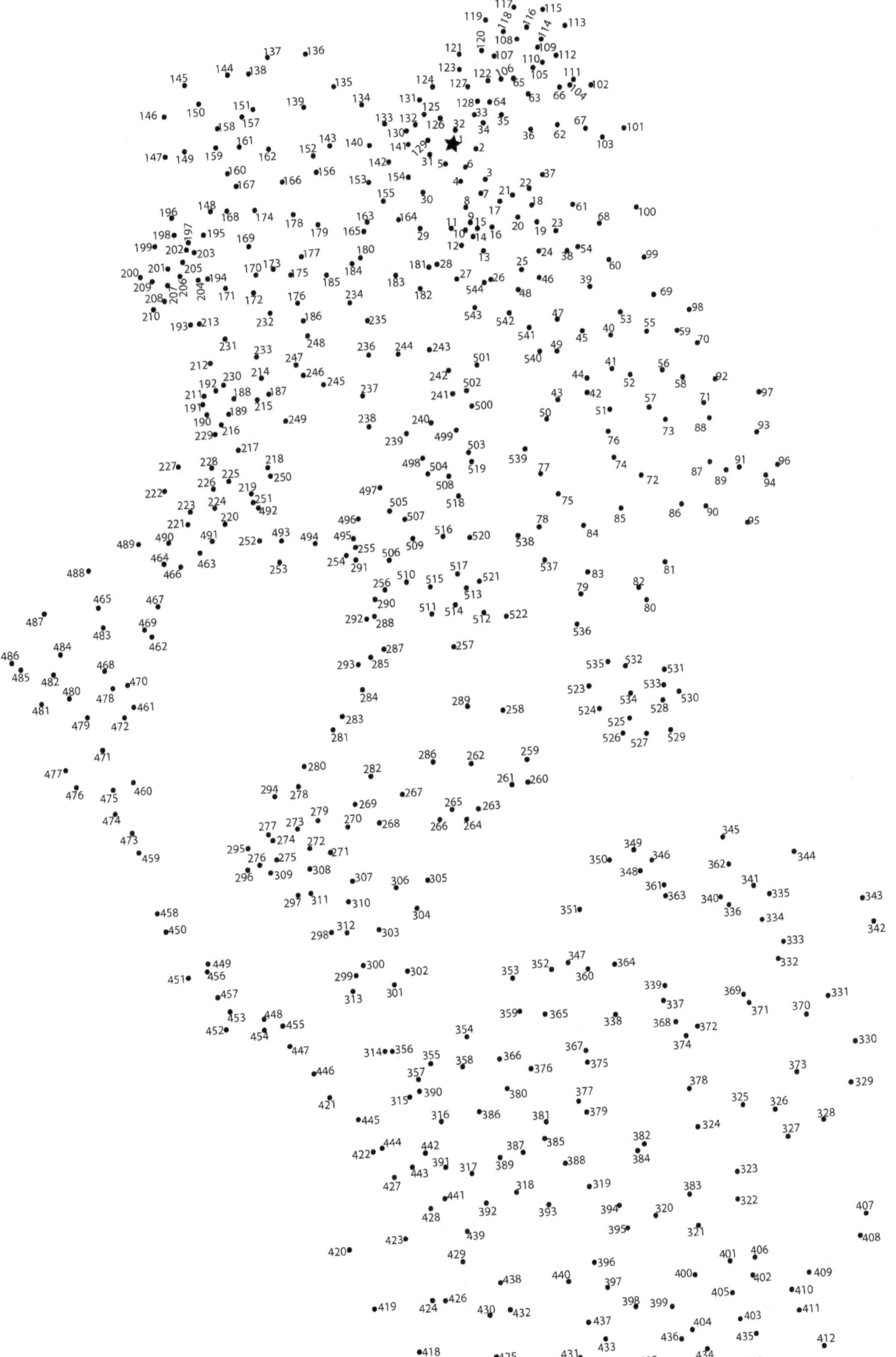

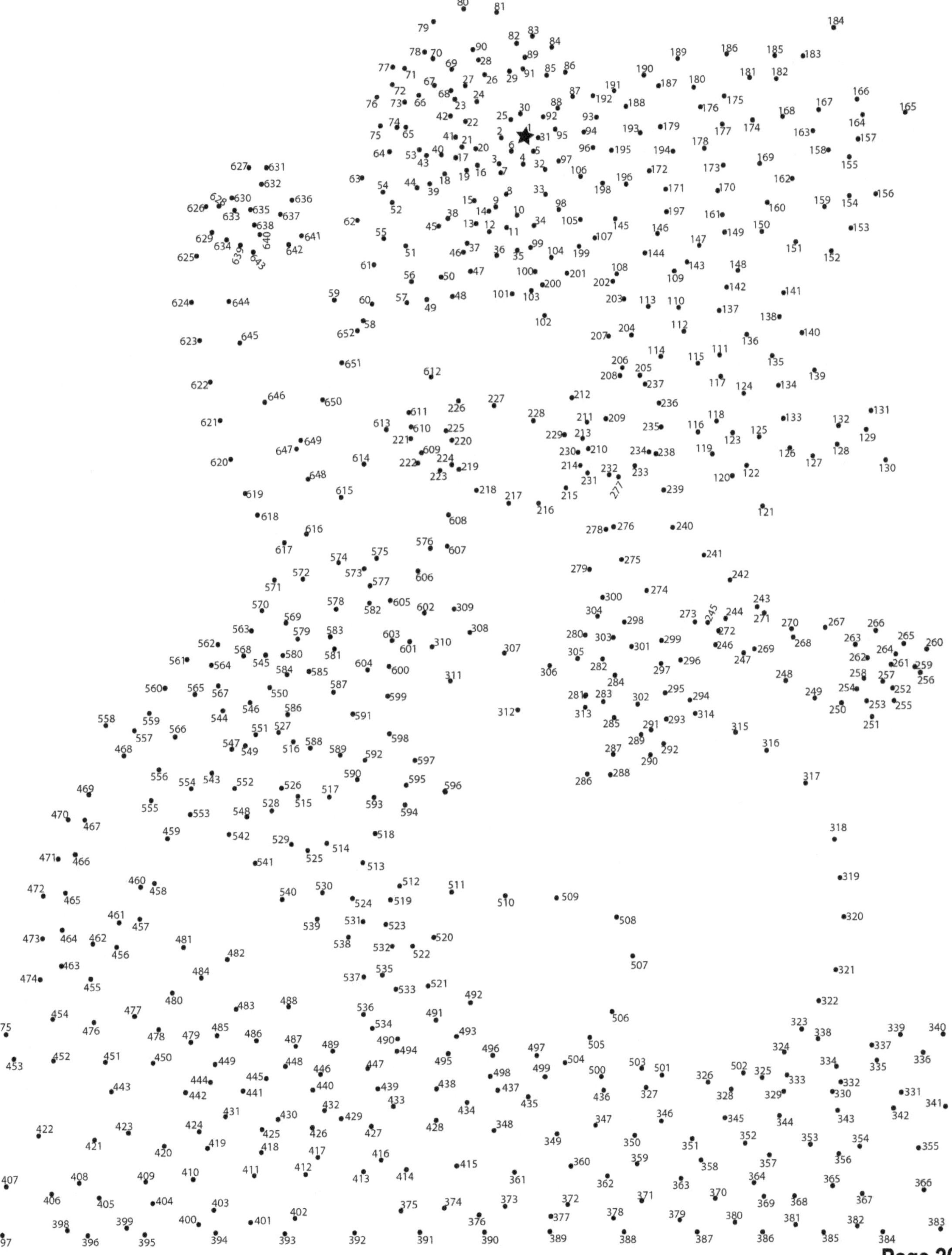

Enjoy bonus images from
some of our other fun
dot-to-dot books

Find all of our books on Amazon

Large Print Dot-to-Dot Sea Life
Puzzles From 150 to 433 Dots

Relaxing Romance By the Ocean
Dot-to-Dot For Adults

46 45 47 53 40 44 57 39 38 41 52 54 37 48 56 3 4 42 51 58 2 7 36 43 49 59 62 8 6 5 20 34 55 10 35 50 60 61 63 13 23 11 30 33 429 428 15 19 21 31 64 67 16 18 29 32 66 68 17 22 28 23 25 27 69 83 26 70 24 85 86 71 82 84

430 427 431 443 432 442 426 433 441 434 440 425 435 439 424 436 438 421 437 423 420 422 393 419 416 415 418 417 392 394 389 390 391 225 395 388 226 413 396 414 354 412 227 237 238 362 387 234 236 240 397 228 235 241 242 243 366 401 245 244 400 386 232 246 247 403 411 229 252 251 249 402 398 230 257 248 405 231 250 256 258 404 399 253 255 384 385 254 259 409 260 261 262 383 382 381 380 277 279 378 330 331 332 328 326 327 320 319 318 313 314 309 308 307 305 304 303

88 215 87 216 214 217 218 213 219 220 212 211 210 209 174 208 207 206 205 172 173 192 204 203 202 175 191 200 193 201 194 189 190 199 177 198 195 176 188 178 196 180 197 182 179 187 181 183 184 186 185 266 267 269 268 270 272 274 273 275 276 280 281 282 283 284 285 286 287 288 289 290 291 292 293 294 295 296 297 298 302 301 299 300 311 312 310

110 112 113 114 105 109 107 90 115 104 108 111 116 138 103 135 136 132 117 119 139 134 131 133 118 120 102 130 129 127 122 140 101 141 142 128 126 123 100 92 125 124 99 91 93 143 90 94 95 98 97 144 167 166 169 168 145 146 165 170 147 148 164 149 163 150 162 151 160 152 154 159 153 155 156 157 158 171

349 350 351 352 353 355 356 357 348 359 358 347 360 361 363 346 367 364 365 345 369 370 344 371 343 373 342 341 374 375 376 377 379 278 329 339 340 338 337 336 334 333 335 325 324 322 321 317 323 316 315 372 264 263 265 271 73 72 81 78 77 74 76 222 75 80 79 223 224 221 226

Follow along with the
page numbers from top left
to bottom right

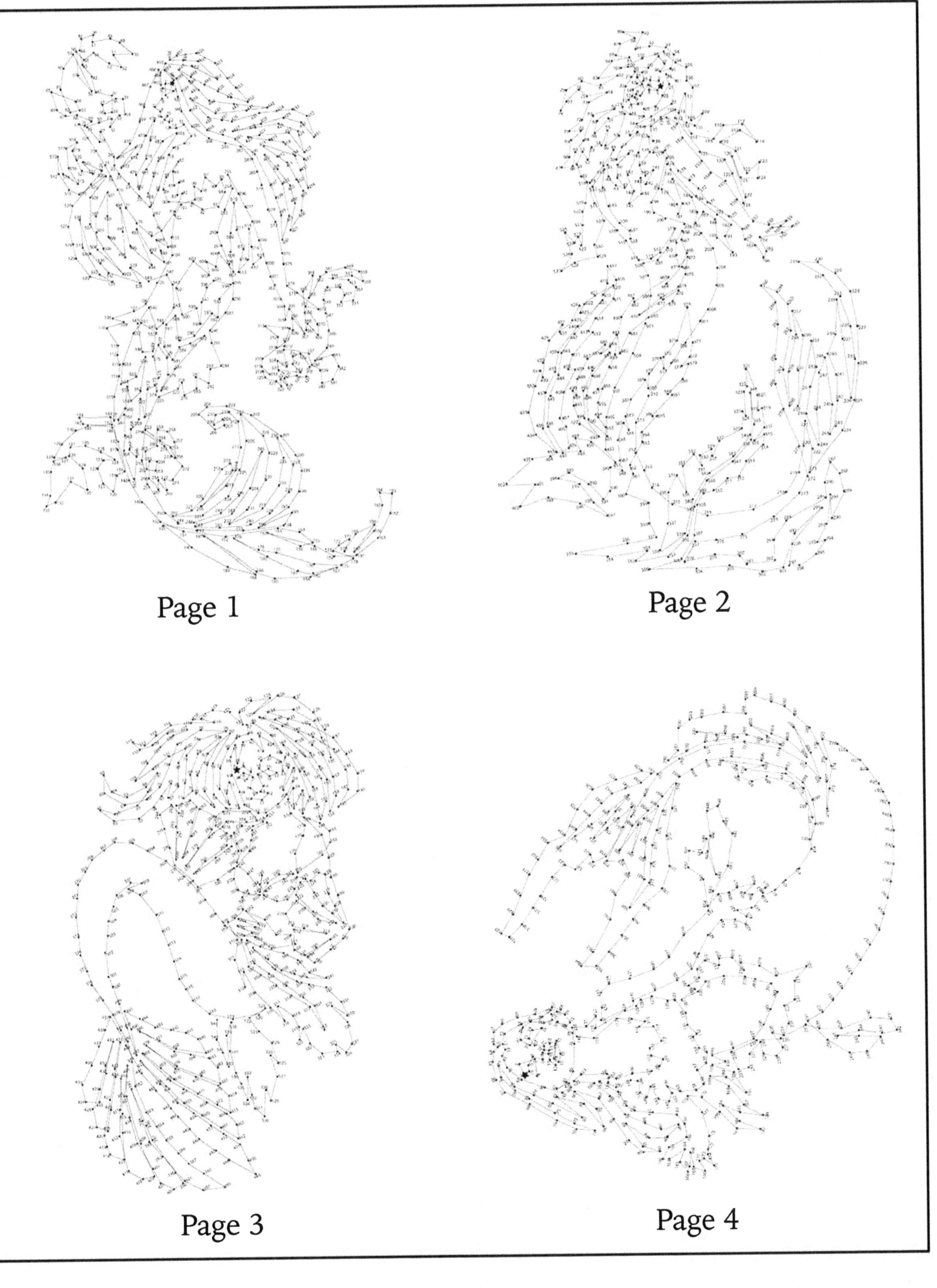

Page 1

Page 2

Page 3

Page 4

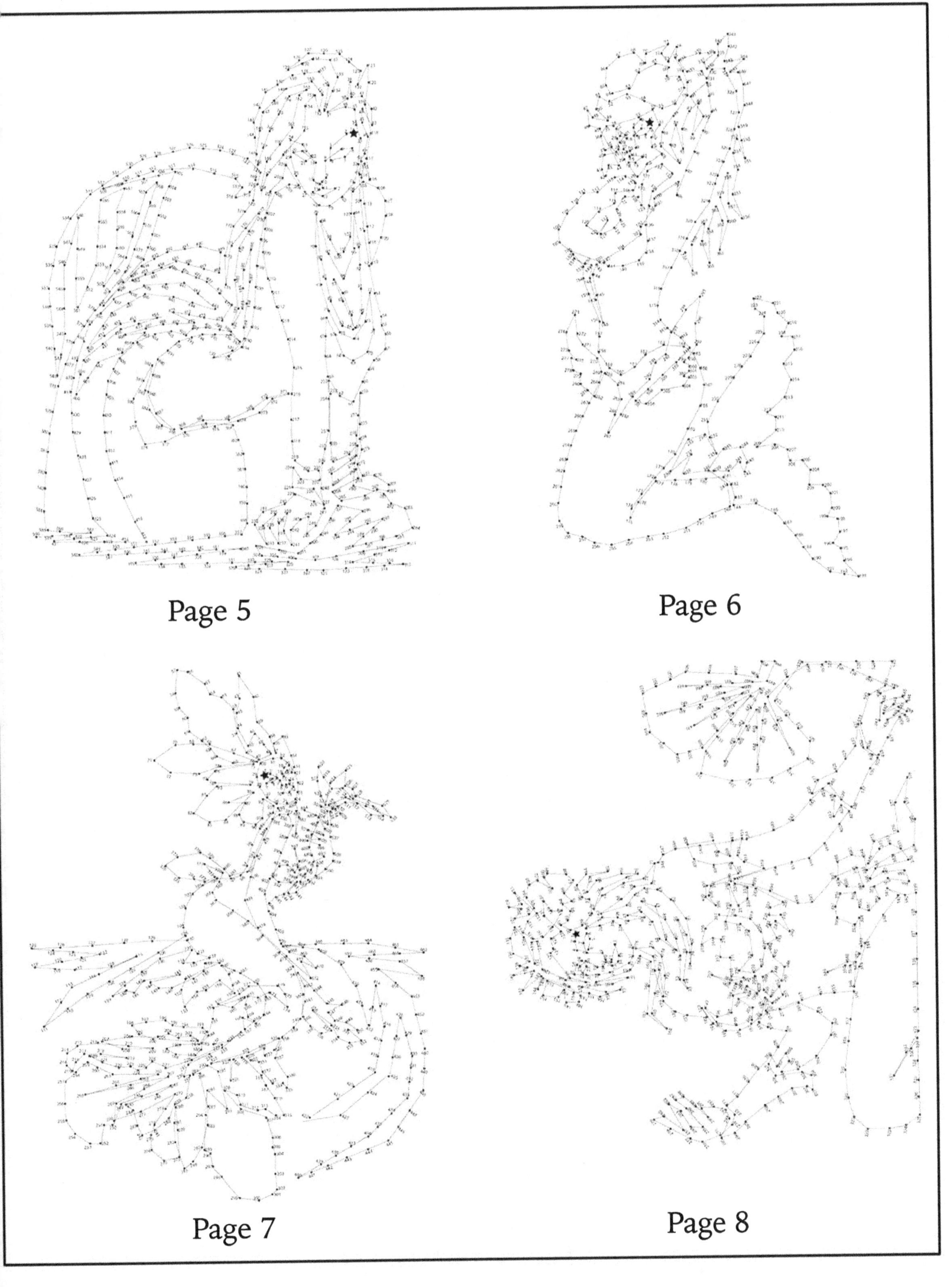

Page 5

Page 6

Page 7

Page 8

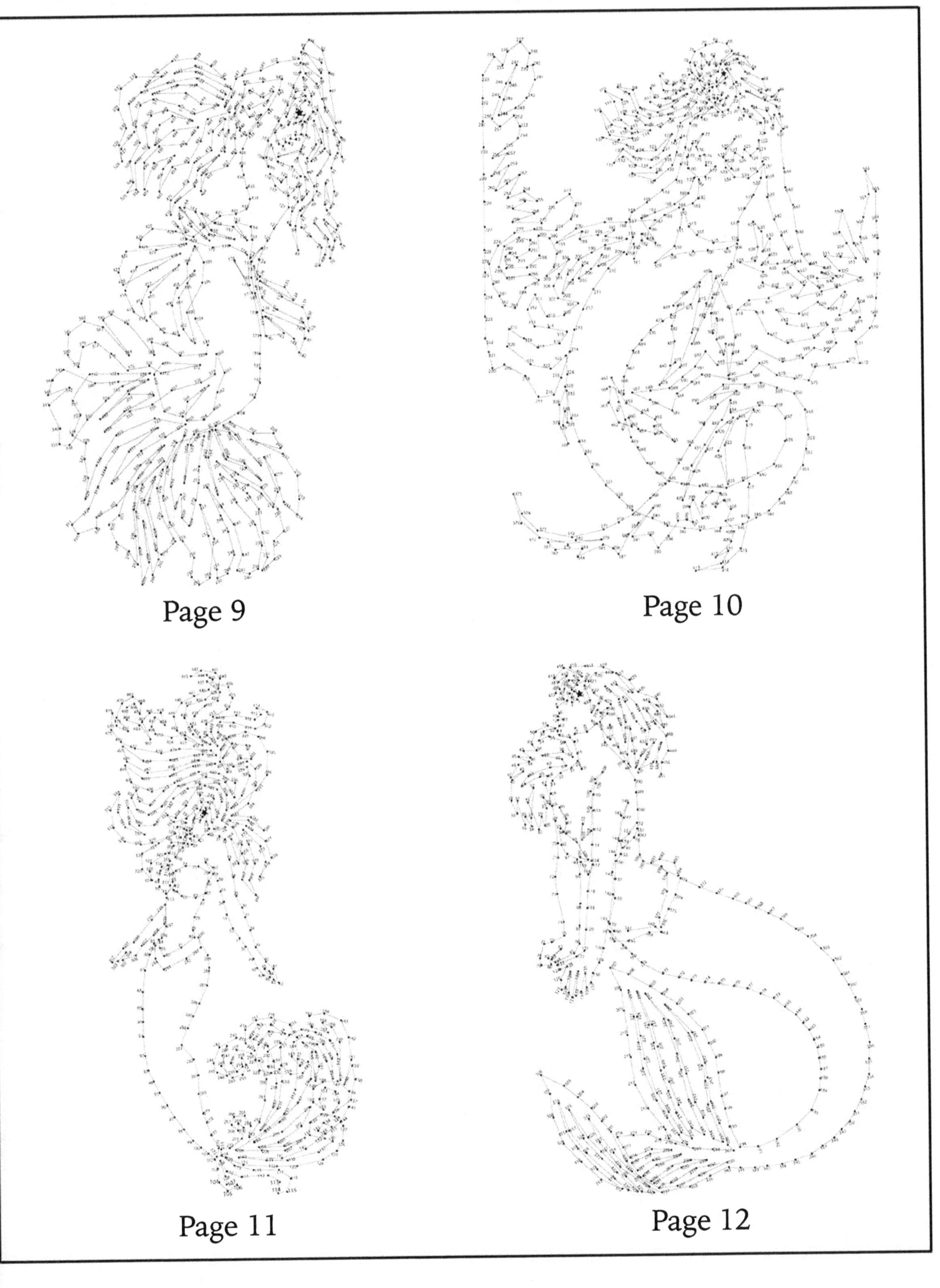

Page 9

Page 10

Page 11

Page 12

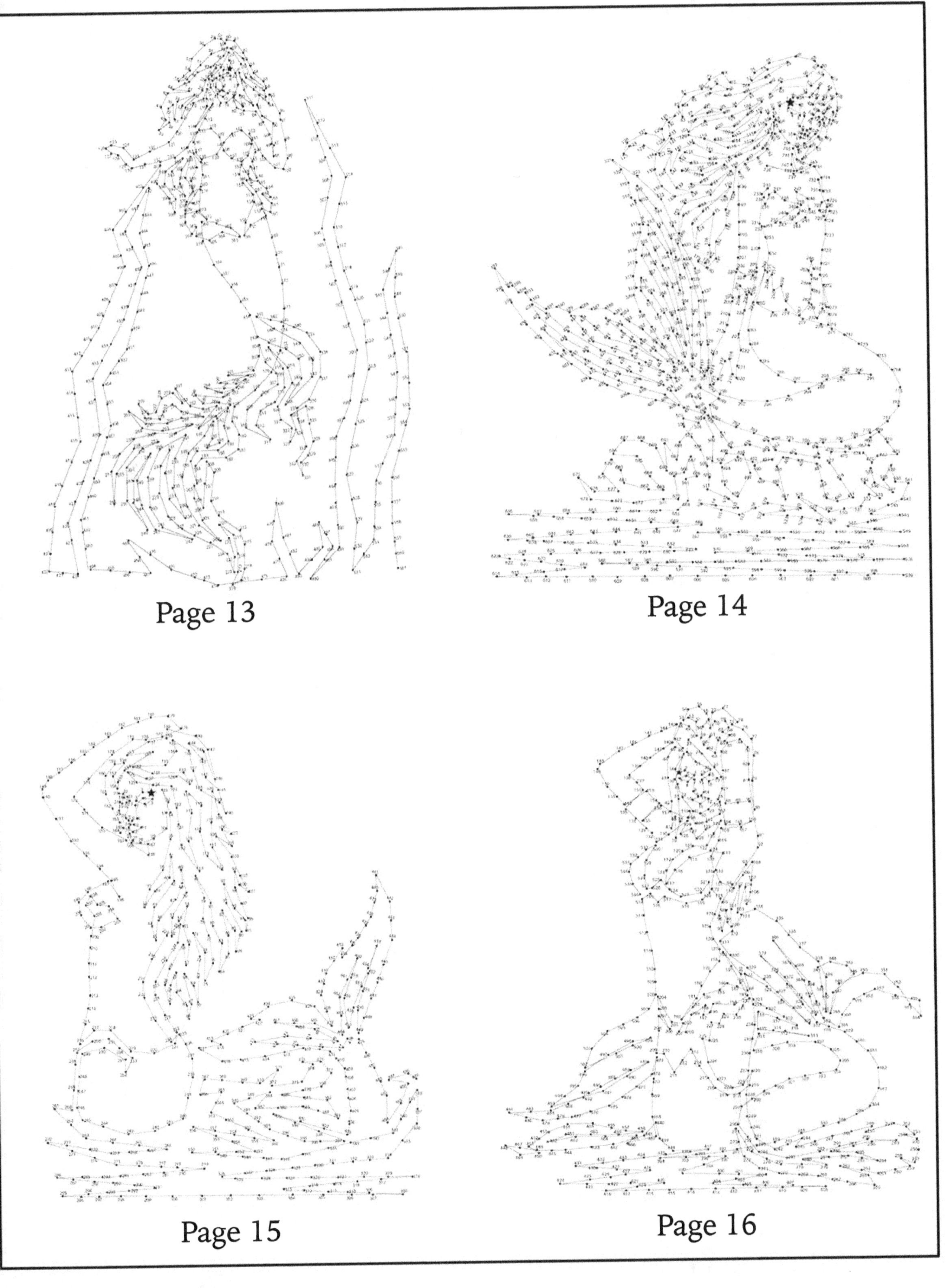

Page 13
Page 14
Page 15
Page 16

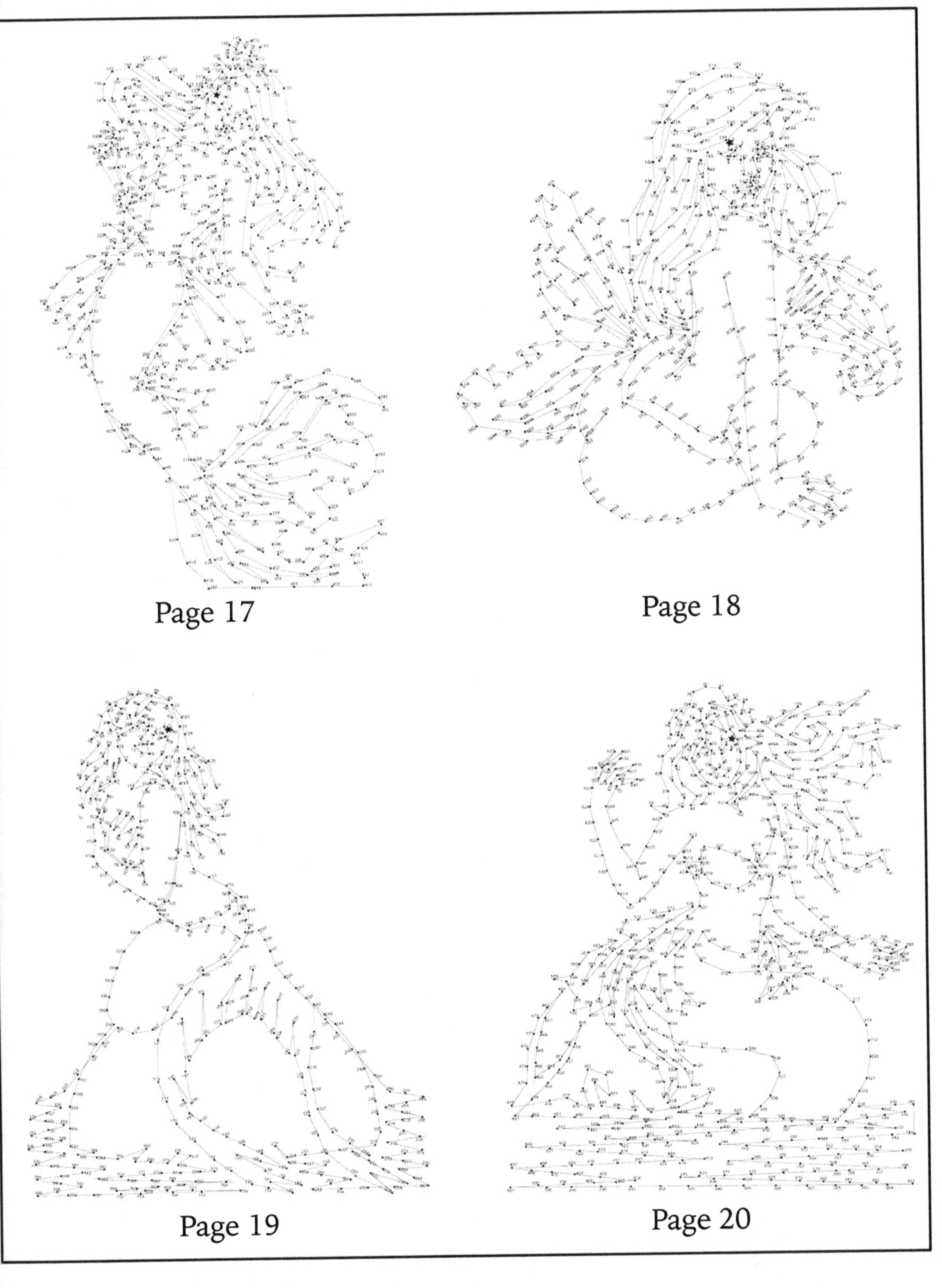

Page 17

Page 18

Page 19

Page 20

Please
Leave
Us
A Review
On Amazon